Bury My Heart at Fun-Fun Mountain

Other FoxTrot Books by Bill Amend

FoxTrot
Pass the Loot
Black Bart Says Draw
Eight Yards, Down and Out

Anthologies

FoxTrot: The Works
FoxTrot en masse

Bury My Heart at Fun-Fun Mountain

A FoxTrot Collection
by Bill Amend

Andrews and McMeel
A Universal Press Syndicate Company
Kansas City

FoxTrot is distributed internationally by Universal Press Syndicate.

Bury My Heart at Fun-Fun Mountain copyright © 1993 by Universal Press Syndicate. All rights reserved. Printed in the United States of America. No part of this book may be used or reproduced in any manner whatsoever without written permission except in the case of reprints in the context of reviews. For information write Andrews and McMeel, a Universal Press Syndicate Company, 4900 Main Street, Kansas City, Missouri 64112.

ISBN: 0-8362-1706-3

Library of Congress Catalog Card Number: 92-74803

Printed on recycled paper

5

8

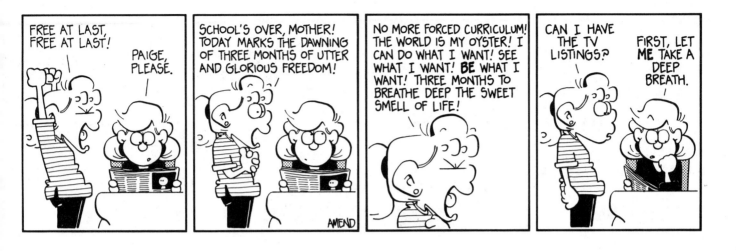

13

18

SO PAIGE IS REALLY SERIOUS ABOUT WRITING SHORT STORIES?

APPARENTLY.

GOOD FOR HER.

SHE'S ALREADY WORKING ON HER SECOND.

I NEVER SAW THE FIRST ONE. WHAT WAS IT ABOUT?

IT WAS TITLED "A DAY AT THE MALL."

AND SHE KEPT IT **SHORT**?

WELL (OOF), SHE ANTICIPATED THERE'D BE SOME EDITING...

AMEND

With the strength of ten men, Sir Galahunk thrust his mighty sword deep into the dragon's belly.

His battle over, the reptile dead, the lone knight headed west through the forest toward his castle.

It was then, in a clearing, that he saw her. Golden hair, twinkling blue eyes... Only two words entered Galahunk's mind.

MOM, IS "HUBBA HUBBA" HYPHENATED?

PAIGE, YOU KNOW, YOU **DO** HAVE A DICTIONARY.

AMEND

There, in the shadows of the forest, Galahunk and the princess fell madly in love.

As the sun set, they kissed. It was for each their first kiss. That magic kiss. The kiss that feels like...

feels like...

YOU REALLY DON'T **KNOW**?

SCREAM IT, WHY DON'T YOU?!

QUINCY'LL SHOW YOU...

AMEND

20

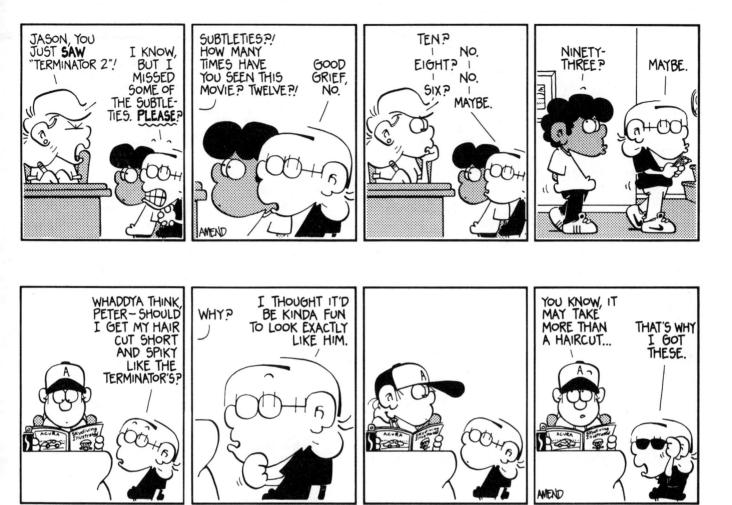

28

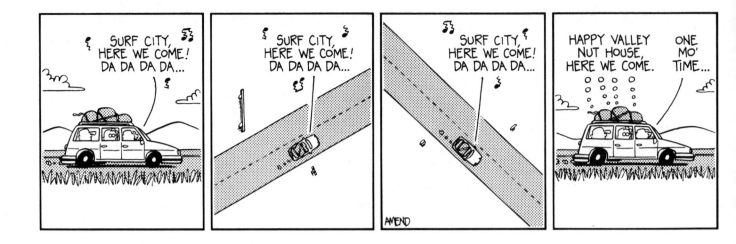

33

39

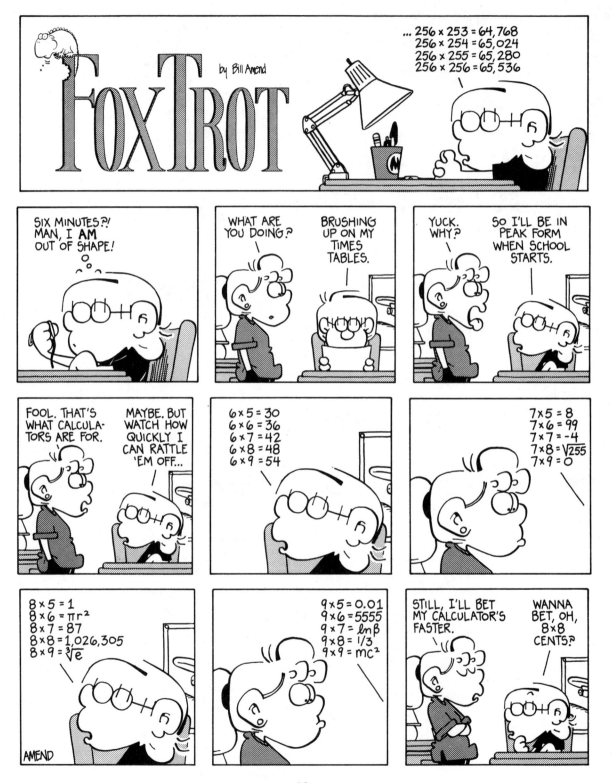

42

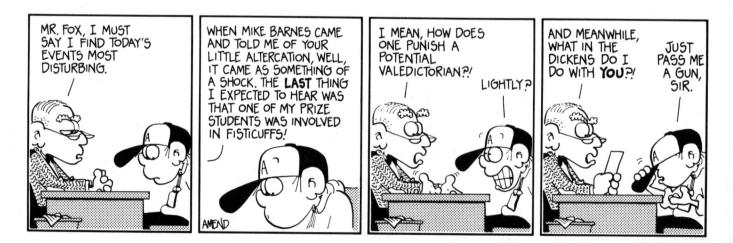

48

50

51

57

62

66

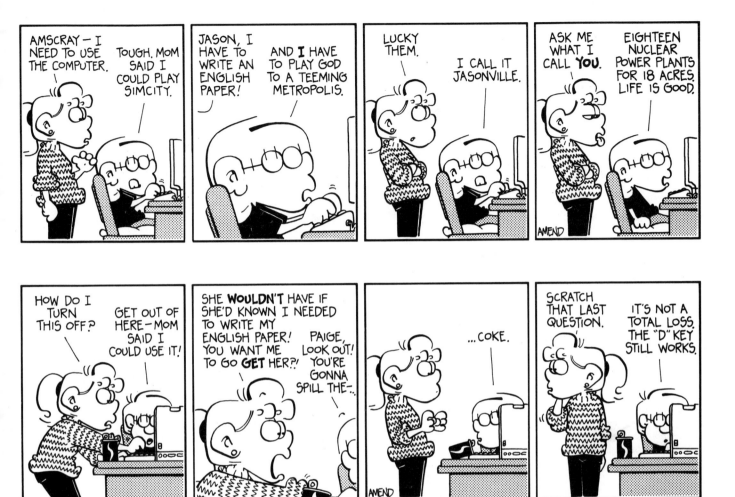

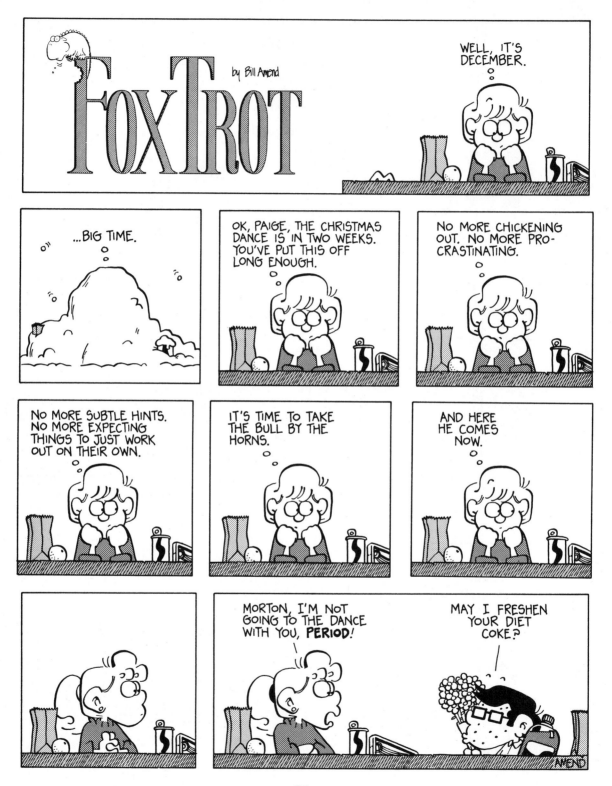

84

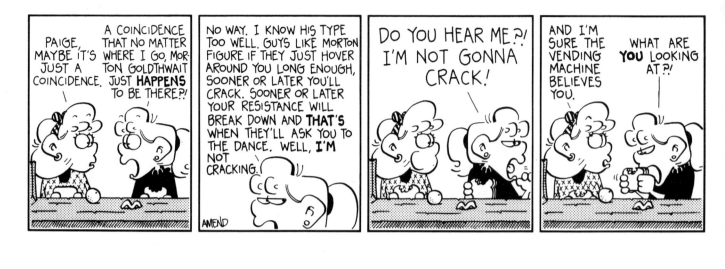

89

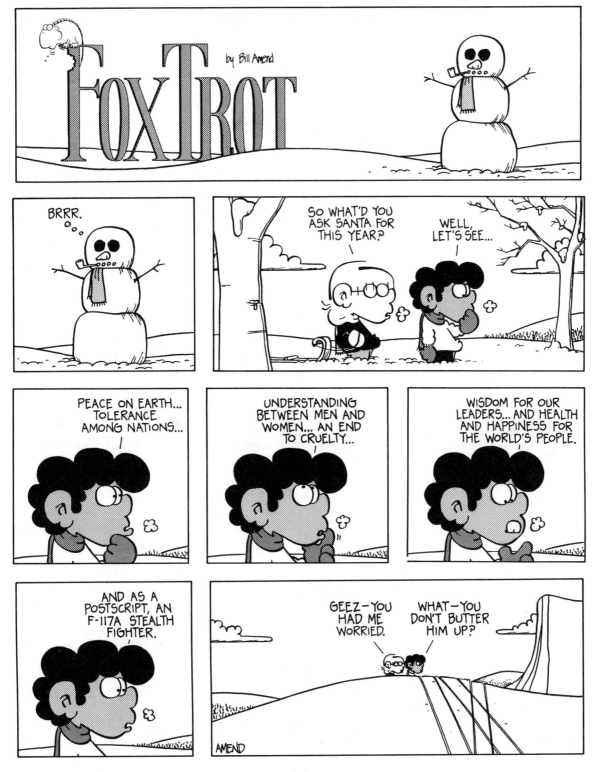

91

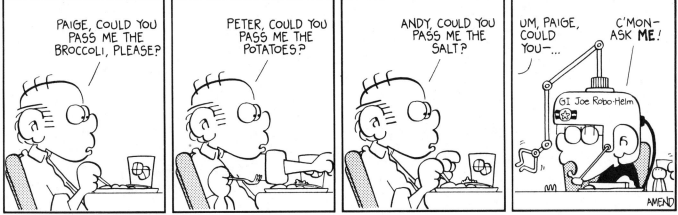

95

98

107

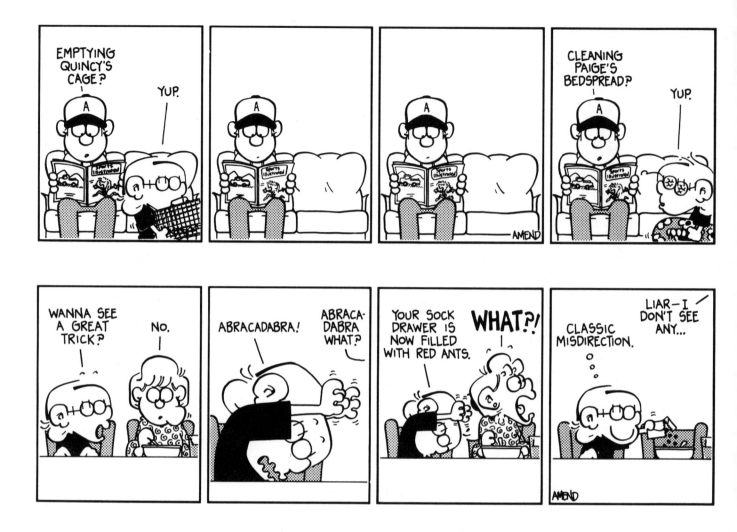

111

116

117

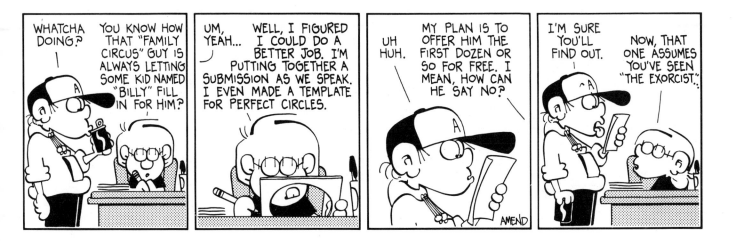

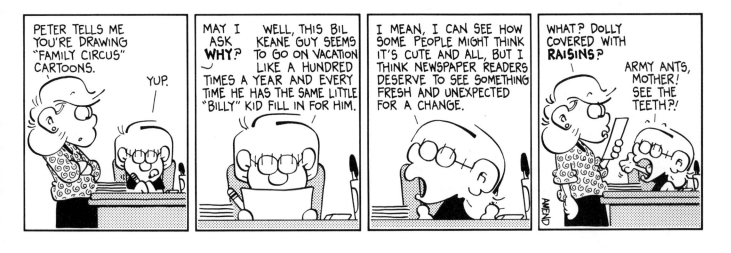